OTHERWISE

Phoenix Poets

A SERIES EDITED BY ROBERT VON HALLBERG

ELEANOR WILNER

# OTHERWISE

THE UNIVERSITY OF CHICAGO PRESS
*Chicago and London*

ELEANOR WILNER lives in Philadelphia. Her two earlier books in the Phoenix Poets series, *Shekhinah* and *Sarah's Choice*, have been hailed for their feminist revisions of Western myth and biblical tradition.

The University of Chicago Press, Chicago 60637
The University of Chicago Press, Ltd., London
© 1993 by The University of Chicago
All rights reserved. Published 1993
Printed in the United States of America
02 01 00 99 98 97 96 95 94 93   1 2 3 4 5

ISBN: 0-226-90029-0 (cloth)   0-226-90030-4 (paper)


Library of Congress Cataloging-in-Publication Data

Wilner, Eleanor.
    Otherwise / Eleanor Wilner.
        p.  cm. —(Phoenix poets)
    I. Title. II. Series.
    PS3573.I45673O84  1993
    811'.54—dc20          92-18038
                            CIP

*To my father, Bernard E. Rand, whose example suggested that when two roads diverge, you can take them both.*

# Contents

Acknowledgments · ix

Prelude

Night Fishing in the Sound · 3

**one**   From the Other Side

Being as I Was, How Could I Help... · 7
When Asked to Lie Down on the Altar · 10
Ume: Plum · 13
Amelia · 17
Saving the Images · 21
Recurrence in Another Tongue: Homage to "Tristia"
    and Osip Mandelstam · 23
The Walls · 26
Admonition · 32
Small Passage between Eons · 33
The Love of What Is Not · 35
    1. Cityscape
    2. E.T., I.U., and That Old-Time Religion
Operations: Desert Shield, Desert Storm · 40
Bat Cave · 44

**two**   *Variations on the Ides of March*

*The Bird in the Laurel's Song* · *51*
*Afterwards* · *53*
*How to Get in the Best Magazines* · *55*
*The Muse* · *58*
*Out of the Hellespont* · *60*
*Leda's Handmaiden* · *63*
*Ambition* · *66*
*The Lament of the Valkyrie* · *71*
*After the Snow Queen Lost Her Charm* · *74*
*"…as soft and as pink as a nursery…"* · *80*
*The Secret Garden* · *83*
*Last Words* · *85*
*Fears about the Moon* · *88*
*Those Who Come After* · *91*

**three**   *Vistas*

*Generic Vision, 1991* · *95*
*Atget's Gardens* · *97*
*Demolition* · *99*
*What Was Left Over* · *101*
*Moonsnails* · *105*
*Freed from Another Context* · *108*
*Remedios Varo as Daphne* · *111*
*The Mulch* · *114*
*Recantation* · *116*
*Kazuko's Vision* · *118*
*American Painting, with Rain* · *120*
*Changing the Imperatives* · *124*

*Notes* · *127*

# Acknowledgments

Thanks are due to the editors of the following periodicals, in which the following poems, several in different versions, originally appeared:

*Boulevard*: "Moonsnails," "Being as I Was, How Could I Help...," "Generic Vision, 1991"

*Calyx, A Journal of Art and Literature by Women*: "Bat Cave" (originally "Return to Bali") (vol. 13:2, summer 1991)

*Caprice*: "Saving the Images," "Recantation" (originally "The Righteous Recant")

*Chicago Literary Review* (the undergraduate literary magazine at the University of Chicago): "Remedios Varo as Daphne"

*Hawaii Review*: "Ambition"

*Indiana Review*: "Those Who Come After," "Kazuko's Vision," "Out of the Hellespont"

*The Kenyon Review*: "Leda's Handmaiden" (New Series, Spring 1990, vol. XII, no. 2; © 1990 by Kenyon College)

*Ms.*: "The Muse"

*Pets and Their People*: "Small Passage between Eons" (issue no. 3, March/April 1989)

*PN Review* (England): "When Asked to Lie Down on the Altar," "What Was Left Over"

*Prairie Schooner*: "Amelia," "American Painting, with Rain," "Demolition," "How to Get in the Best Magazines," "The Mulch," "Recurrence in Another Tongue," "The Walls." Reprinted from *Prairie Schooner* by permission of the University of Nebraska Press. Copyright © 1993 University of Nebraska Press.

*Rain City Review*: "Afterwards," "Last Words"

*Southwest Review*: "Night Fishing in the Sound"

*TriQuarterly* (a publication of Northwestern University): "*Ume*: Plum," "Atget's Gardens," "Changing the Imperatives"

My thanks to the John D. and Catherine T. MacArthur Foundation, whose Fellowship helped in the completion of this manuscript.

I am grateful for the enlivening companionship of the present and former students and my colleagues at the Warren Wilson MFA Program for Writers. And to D. M. Ranney, Ruth Kennedy, and all the women of "Portfolio," my mother's writing friends, whose example mattered more than they knew.

*Prelude*

# Night Fishing in the Sound

The sound is dark; you can barely hear
the gauze-wrapped warning song
of bells, and cannot see
the buoys swinging on top
the oily waves, the water a black
so absolute it drinks light
back, unquenchable thirst
like that the shades in Hades had
for the hot blood of sacrifice—
how the dead swell, like ticks,
till they rise, bloated envoys
out of the envious dark.

The waves of the sound sway
endlessly, a restless channel caught
between two seas—one fresh, the other salt—
as if suspended between hope and
certain sorrow. And you, in a small craft,
having left behind the little inland
sea, are tossed in all this roiling dark;
the trick is to play the wind
for time, sinking the line
deep into the heaving black, trying
not to stare at the dizzying lantern swinging
over the deck, a drunken sun on a pendulum;

trying to keep your equilibrium
with no horizon to steady the eye, riding
the dark sound blind, hoping for fish,
wanting to reel in, to reach the end
of the passage, but afraid
of the waiting ocean, the enormous dawn
when light, rising from below, seems to come
from everywhere at once, tsunami of
overwhelming sun.

But still there is
the solid feel of the helm
under your hand, worn grain
of wood that fits the grasp
and steers the little craft
out of the rocking cradle of the dark,
safe, into the cauldron of dawn.

**o n e**        *From the Other Side*


He would cry out on life, that what it wants
Is not its own love back in copy-speech,
But counter-love, original response.

—Robert Frost, from "The Most of It"

# Being as I Was, How Could I Help...

It was the noise that drew me first,
even before the scent. The long water
had brought something to my den, spilling
its banks, leaving the hollow pod
of reeds in the cool mud. Whatever it was,
it cried inside, and an odor rose
from it—man-smell but sweeter.
Two small hairless cubs were in it, pink
as summer oleander, waving
the little worm-like things they had
instead of paws. Naked like that, they
made my blood go slow, my dugs
begin to drip. I tipped the pod, they slid
into the ferns, I nuzzled the howling
pair, they found my side, they suckled
there and drank their fill. That night
the red star in the sky was bright,
a vulture's eye that waits
with a patience that I hardly understand.
The twin cubs slept in their shining
skin, warm at my side. I dreamed:

The trees were falling, one by one,
the sound deafening, the dust that rose
from one a mist to hide the felling
of the next. The mountains were
cut in two; great stones were rolled
and piled like hills until the sky
was shut; where the trees
had grown, pillars of stone rose
high, the birds circled, but
their skulls struck the sky.
Teeth chewed the earth; our den fell in
like a rotted log when weight is
added to decay; nothing to eat, the cubs
howled, the flesh fell from our bones,
we ran under a strange sky whose light
was wrong: it rose from the city walls,
bounced off the leaden heaven—flat
as the sound of a stone striking mud.
One of the brothers killed the other.
Blood poured where the streams had run.

Nowhere to drink, we slink from one rock
to the next; hunger drives us to the walls
where, sharp as the eyes of men, death
waits with its thousand iron thorns.

But the warm sun woke me. I forgot.
The twins were all I saw; for days
we lay together by the den, the river
ran beside us like a friend; they drank
and laughed at the morning light
that played in the shelter
of the leaves. Forgive me,
I was wolf, and could not help
the love that flowed from me to them,
the thin sweet river of milk.
Even now, though the world has come
to match the dream, I think
I would give it again.

# When Asked to Lie Down
# on the Altar

—for Marie Howe, and her "Isaac"

A guiding hand raised
above us, haloed in sun, the glint
of silver on the blade like the sheen
of sperm...
                    there was the boy,
tadpole swimming upriver, a miracle
about to unravel again, the birth
a matter (each time) of amazement,
and there, on the hill, as always,
sharpening his knife, the sad man
with the headache, the servants,
the high opinion of himself, the sand
it was built on, the mountain
his stand-in—raising its stones
toward the heavens, straining against the rain,
the wind, the merciless years that were wearing it
down, inexorably, the undulant way
that stone is worn
by the tongue of the rivers...
                              so, lowering himself
on the woman—the pride of his flocks, the power
of his tents in his member—he launches
this Isaac, tail still thrashing, who
grows in that inland sea where

the children of deserts lie down in still
waters, and there, in the placid place
of beginning, rock in the haven of dark.

Back on that mountain, the cold
dry air of an unforgiving
climate, the father
forces the animal onto the stone,
and now, the sun draws nearer,
the sweat pours into our eyes
and blurs our sight, so we can no longer
tell which is the boy Isaac, which is
the ram, for when the man
looks down he sees, in the face
of the boy looking up at him, the wet
eyes of the uncomprehending sheep, and
as he buries his fingers in the ram's
deep wool, he feels the bony shoulders
of his son, and everywhere (is it
the heat?) the world swims in red, and
his hands, the stones, the altar, the split
side of the mountain, the curve of the earth
run with it, the rivers are stained
with it, the tides are a strange burnt
umber, the waves wash into the shores
the color of rusted iron, the red
of a knife that has lost its edge,
that has spent years exposed
to the rain, so when you reach
to pick it up, it crumbles in your hand
like a cake of dried mud, and the air
picks up the grains of it, moving
them in slow spirals of dust

and smoke, sending them
like signals toward
a lost tribe
in a buried village
of tents folded like the wings
of dead moths
under the burned out lamp
of heaven.

And it wasn't a lamb, but the strong ram
of manhood we dreamed, women
dipping our urns again and again
into the darkening well;
                              it was not a son
but the man himself we lost, the man
who sacrificed what might have been
to his fear, and who came home
a stranger to the tent
smelling of blood
and the death
of what we had stayed for,
late, after the others
had given up hope,
after the others
had changed
to receive him.

# Ume: *Plum*

The fruit is small, and often served
shriveled, soaked in some attar or
other, an odd shade of red, weak and
toward the blue. Sometimes one
of these unpromising tiny plums
is set in the center
of a flat bed of white rice, to mime
the nation's flag—red sun
on a white field. Those years ago, we never
knew, kept ignorant of all that might
disable war, that the flag with the wide
red rays, that rose over the bodies,
adorned the Zero's wings, was a war flag,
emblem of a burning sun, like rage
or whatever it is that sets men's lives
at nought, and pours them, young
and hot, down history's drain.

The trees here must be bred for the beauty
of their flower, for the plums are sour, the cherries
small and bitter—but, oh, the *ume* blooming

in the early spring, the *sakura* unfolding
in a brilliant sky, blossoms borrowing
the light for shelter, a glowing parasol
of pink and white, or
the world a child's globe
that sits in the Buddha's hand
and when he laughs, it shakes, until
the air is filled with silken snow,
the wind toying with it, lifting
the petals as if back to the branch,
then bringing them lightly down.

Walking the shimmering tunnel of flowering
trees along the Imperial moat, Mrs. Nakano
and I spoke of the war, when we were
both children (the same age, I think,
though it was a point of pride with her
to never say). Her voice was
matter-of-fact, or else it was
the way English goes flat in a mouth
made for another tongue.
In Kobe, she had crouched with her
mother in the bomb shelter while our
planes bombed her city flat. The trees
shivered a little, the delicate arbor
sent down a shower of petals
to our feet. The carp, grown huge, slid by
in the moat, and the rain began, steady;
we opened our umbrellas
as we went. She spoke then
about her husband, her misery
with him, his anger and his mother,
the doors that one by one
she'd tried and found them locked.

How do we keep from going mad? I thought, looking
at the trees bred for their beauty
by an aesthetic breed of men, who
wanted a woman wrapped in tissue-thin silk,
her mouth a hole with blackened teeth,
who would dive at the dark stack of a ship
to a fiery death. And saw, with them, our own
young men, the same, filing into the black
belly of a huge cargo plane, each with a woman
in his wallet, her words on lilac paper,
her distant image as his aphrodisiac
in hell. I tried to ask the question that can't
be asked in words—having no subject and no predicate
but death. I thought of the bombs falling, and
then my mind went blank as the radar screen
when the thing that moves into its range
is much too close, or gone.

And Mrs. Nakano and I, the fortunate ones,
walked side by side beneath the cherry trees
and watched the great smoking craters
of memory fill in and disappear, and watched
the rain turn the fallen petals
into a sticky debris, and walked
because we were alive, and walked
to keep from going mad, and walked
for beauty, and for company,
the whole perimeter of the Emperor's moat,
that carp-infested fence around
the palace, walled in,
where power keeps its face,

and ends, as history ends, in Lear—
old, heartsore, the dead
Cordelia in his arms. Reverse pietà,
a motherless world, the father
holding the sacrificed child
on a ground of fallen petals
wet with rain, plum
on a field of white.

But here, we break the circle, cross
the street, and bow.
We part, Mrs. Nakano
and I, go, each
to her own
gate.

# *Amelia*

We had lived centuries apart. The imperial
soul had its gardens, far from home, where
fancy held its court, fiction made its peace,
lost horizons, sunless caverns, miles
from where the gleaming pearls of spit
lay in the unpaved streets—those seething seas
of mud or tunnels of dust; twin buckets
across the shoulders on a yoke, the slosh
of night soil going to the fields
to coax the rice through the steaming paddies'
mirrors, to fill a hunger we could not
have dreamed. The jangle of coins that buys
only the smell of meat. On the market table's block
the pig's head leers, its eyes like marbles
lost in a haze of flies; nearby the baskets
of dried scorpions, medicinal skins of snake—
a lifetime shed, a landing strip is
suddenly kleig-lit: Madame Chiang
Kai-shek smiling in the newsreel film,
stepping delicately down the silver stairs
of a shining plane to America, her arms
laden with roses; her body chic
and slim in a sheath of Chinese silk,
her English as smooth, impeccable.

What did we know
of the river near Chongqing
filling with bodies like a human soup;
what did we know of the people
marching north, burning with ideals,
brilliant Mao with his almost female face,
his growing force a pincers to pull
the rotten tooth of Chiang Kai-shek
from China's aching mouth. What
did we know—nice American kids
wearing the tinted glasses that
Dorothy wore to dim the glare
of Oz, green fire from a lake
of burning ice. How we yearned to be Madame
Chiang Kai-shek, cool, clicking her mahjong
tiles, enchanted, a distant song, elusive
as the other who flew through the pages of *LIFE*—
brave Amelia, remember? the woman who fell
from the skies. Amelia Earhart, lost in flight,
all the lost years ago.
                    Through one we ruled,
by proxy, but through Amelia we lived,
around some distant river's
idle bend, in dense forests
where no sign of mangled craft
was ever found. So few paths to choose—
we chose those two: the one who flew away
and fell from sight; the other
one—the General's wife.

The General's wife has long since been
disgraced, the silk veil torn, the fist
with its painted nails pried apart.
But Amelia lives on, as real
to us as Arthur was
to the English tribe who dreamed
of his return. Our distant hope
careens across the skies—spy
satellite that spins and scans
the lush Pacific isles—until below,
what is that gleam? Adjust the focus
of the close-up lens, and watch
(among the layered masks of green
the island wears) the image grow
and clear: shed carapace
of steel and cast-off wings; nearby,
a woman moving by the tangled bank
along the stream. And being still
American, we see her in a beam
of light, alone, in all the secrecy
of public glare, the dream itself
a bit theatrical.
                    She stops to gaze
into the pool where stones have
steadied the water for self-portraiture:
she sees her hair, grown long and white,
a shimmering face that smiles
through a network of lines. "Lost
for good," she thinks, and smiles back,
then takes a step aside. The second
her image is gone, she sees

the scene grown suddenly wide, a world
of green, profuse and noisy with life:
the hum of hives and villages,
the flowers with their open, lurid lives,
the insect drone, the chatter of monkeys, constant cry of birds,
and in the water's pause—an overflowing bowl
of sky and scudding clouds.

# Saving the Images

The screen flickers, an old film unwinds
in the grainy black and white
of yesterday's mind—a child, watching,
mystified: the freight train waiting
on the landscape of the war, the shouts
at night, shadows that move like men,
running feet, the train's hoot, the hiss
of steam, the shape of odd French caps,
the fevered haste, the Nazis closing
from the rear, the masterpieces of the Louvre
about to fall into enemy
hands. The distant engines roar,
the time is short, the men are loading
the boxcars—blank squares of art
hustled into the dark, muffled and wrapped
(as if the painted faces could cry out),
shots ring out, the train begins to move...

from years away, I still can hear
the sound of shots, the train
start up, its wheels turn
as it picks up speed, drawing the lens
behind it down the tracks, fixing the eye
on art's grand escape
down the lines to the vanishing
point, leaving the ones who had loaded the cars
splayed on the tracks behind. As if
the distance ahead were the sky above
they seem to be clutching the wooden ties,
climbing the rungs to heaven,
angels crawling like flies
along the fallen Jacob's ladder,
kicked down by a retreating God,
its rails disappearing
into the clouds
of steam
as the music
comes up
and the credits
come on
eye follows
the dust
up a beam of light
to the blinding white
projector's lens—
headlight of an oncoming train.

# Recurrence in Another Tongue: Homage to "Tristia" and Osip Mandelstam

*Noch, úlitsa, fonár, optéka...*
And everything will recur as before
night    street    lamppost    drugstore
—Aleksandr Blok

You can hear the slow methodical chewing
of the oxen, the soft slap
of their lips, the dull grinding
of teeth like the stones that grind wheat
to a fine powder. Like the grain,
I have mastered the art of separation.
I am chaff in the wind; for the rest,
no matter. That was grist for the mill
of Stalin. Such men are the same, they recur.
While, endlessly changing, I am
a glimmer of dust in your lamplight, a flurry
of pollen on the open, illegible
page, an obscure song you can almost
remember, swaying shadows of flame, blank
eyes of a painted, candle-lit saint—
black-centered, staring, almost blind
with vision, with accusation. And the Muse?
Her voice marries the wailing of women:
song    agony    song.

After all, it was going to be a new life.
Remember? Hope wandered the streets
like a drunk, befriending everyone.
What did we know of separation, of the night
coming bareheaded, hat in hand, begging
for another hour of dark? How could we know
of the mornings to follow, when each said
goodbye to the others, for no one knew
who would return in the evening, who would be
taken away? For us, it was dawn. Though
the rooster, herald of the new day,
astride the city wall,
was wildly flapping his wings.
And the oxen, the oxen were grinding
their slow stone jaws.

To sing of the rituals of yarn: the carding, the spindle,
the shuttle, the spinning, the air filled
with furious lint, the silken
dross of the thread, the down
of a swan, the steppes filling with snow—
and barefoot, running always towards us
Delia, whose body the wind sculpts with her dress
into the shape of desire, language
impoverished by bliss.
If everything could recur as before—
for that instant of sweet recognition,
would we suffer it all again?

Nadezdha, who had me by heart, hoarding
my words, running, carrying herself
from one corner of Russia to the other, like an urn
full of ashes, waiting for her chance
to scatter them abroad ... dust, ashes, *noch,*
*úlitsa, fonár, optéka*... a translucent figurine
on a white clay plate, squirrel pelt
nailed flat and spread to dry: effigies
of a century of wax and bronze—we, who could not
have guessed the crowds of dead in the dark
of Erebus, who died foretelling
a great future, women and men alike, thrown
into a common ditch, wax to cast bronze
for the headless statue of our murdered hope.

But the ashes are scattered, the words, a cloud-
burst of wings, the cage doors standing open.
And everything may recur as before
but not these ashes, not this air.

# The Walls

—for Melanie

## 1. THE CHORUS

Do you remember the city where we were born,
the city into which we came
before the garden? The passages,
dazzling intersections, the odd turns,
the light playing over it all,
the city of language—the child with her mouth
open like a bird in the nest,
with hunger, the beginnings of song.
Our song made our place; the words, the city
to which we were born. But the city had
walls, and it was the walls
we tried to scale, as a singer lifts her voice
note by note after that elusive high C;
as the rock climber inches his way, hand
over pick over rock, with infinite care,
over the mile-high cliff wall of granite;
as a fly buzzes its way along the facade
of the skyscraper, story after story,
until its wings droop and it falls
on the sill, exhausted dust.
                              It was the walls
that came with the city of words, and
the walls were of silence. Not the black and

lovely soundlessness of space, nor the absolute
stillness of deer at the slightest
disturbance, nor the vast
silence of plains that stretch beyond
the horizon—no, this was
a vertical silence: what is tall and
comes between. When you try
to get by it, it moves
before you, or after, like a wave
or a following wind; it seems
sometimes the very air
is made of it.

        And though we climb and
climb, it seems to grow with us; and though
we throw ourselves over the fences, as we land
we look up, and they've moved out in front
and again stand before us—
as when a forest
suddenly sprouts a wall of spears,
a tall tribe surrounds us,
their language strange, their
speech our noise, our fear is
their silence. We look in their eyes,
and they look in ours, and we wait.
And it is hard to say who
is the most afraid.

2. CHORUS with
      Hans, the painter
      Miriam, one of the sisters

Chorus, *Vacha, East Germany*

Of course we all spoke German, but
we were always on opposite sides.
In the mind, many can become one thing.
In the world, it is not so.
The wall was always there, as long
as we can remember, built by a past
we hadn't made. No one spoke
of what we yearned to know:
how one tyrant turned
into the next, what dug
the greasy hole called war
into which our missing father
fell. Our mother raised us on the hope
of his return. The wall, cinderblock
topped with barbed wire, stood
in the center of the old stone bridge
that crossed the river Werra.
For years we lived with half a bridge,
with border guards, the river a Styx
that only the dead could cross.
But tonight at 2 A.M. we heard
a crashing like the thunder
of Thor's hammer, or ice breaking up
in the spring—the workers
were smashing the wall to bits,
and a bulldozer finished it. At first light
we'll cross to the other side,
to the village where our mother was born.

*Bryn Mawr, Pennsylvania:*

Hans:    It was early in the game. When
              Hitler first appeared, and ran,
              my parents laughed. I remember how we
              never took him seriously—a small man,
              a ranter with a dog's face, *dreck*,
              a tin-pot bully. Then he won
              the vote. So. Chosen by the multitude,
              a triumph of the general will. A toast
              to the great Rousseau. Hope
              murdered with the rest. Afterwards
              I expected nothing, and laughter
              was my comrade, came easier
              than thought. I worked in a hospital
              for defectives; I had the care
              of a brain-damaged boy. He used
              to masturbate and sing. He made it
              to paradise; I to America.
              I teach art in a wooded college
              for the daughters of the rich. I paint
              over and over the face
              of a clown, its mouth stained red.
              The Berlin wall? Oh that.
              Whatever goes up, comes down.

*Jerusalem*

Miriam:   What is the world? Here in Jerusalem,
          at the Wailing Wall, as always, the cracks
          are filled with messages to God. In
          the hospital Hadassah Ein Kerem
          a dying Arab is saved
          by the transplant of an Israeli's heart,
          a man from Galilee named Traum
          shot in this war of brothers. Both sides
          are up in arms at this, except the Arab's wife.
          Will she leave a prayer folded in the wall?
          Whose heart beats in Jerusalem tonight?

Chorus, *Site of Denver, Colorado*

When we reached the end of the Great Plains
after months of banging over the ruts,
puking out our guts from bad water,
dragging our wagons through mud and swollen
streams, burying our dead along the way
until the Long Trail West was lined
by crosses like signs along a road; when at last
we were at the end of it, the flat expanse
of America, we came to the Great Wall
of the Rockies. They rose before us
like the back of some reclining God, old
and huge beyond our measure,
what had been always
turned away.
                    We would go it alone
from there. We camped to wait for
summer. When the trees greened out,
we would climb to the silent passes,
find our way along the ridge, and cross.

．　　．　　．

But some of us stayed, loving the mountains,
unfolding ourselves like prayers
from the cracks in the wall, and living
in so much silence, and with so long a view—
we forgot
not to be happy, we forgot
what it was
we thought
had stood in the way.

# *Admonition*

You are
their sister. Nevertheless
they accuse you of the worst.
When you defend yourself
they call you
defensive. Beware—
you who traffic with
the wet nurses
of history, those iron nipples,
that acid drink,
pure and deadly.

# Small Passage between Eons

She parted the birds before her as she ran—
spray flung wide from her wet-nosed
prow, whose prowess was all nosing
in the leaves, each pile
a lexicon of rootings and relief
by former stoppers at the spot.
And what she thought, well, we supposed,
who filled her huge, inquiring eyes
with imports philosophical and
wise, imagining a sage's soul
embedded in the body of a hound,
although beneath the ground
of our conceit, a rumbling
growl occasionally arose
from a farther place
than our cerebral tenancy
in time could apprehend, a something
redolent of wolf, and yet more
ancient, primitive and vast—
tucked into the recess
of her mind, like a small explosive
in an envelope, that opening will detonate
and our neat order shatter, time
go all at once into abeyance,

waiting to begin again its usual
forward march; and there, behind
the long white bones
of those incisors bared,
a lush primeval place, a kingdom
neither peaceable nor good
but at the center of the sacred wood
where blood is shed as casually
as tears, long-legged cats
stalk trembling mice with joy
and the tiny shrew with huge eyes
hunts the night, slaughtering insects
in a fevered haste, or worms
to fuel its small ferocious heat—
it burns to eat, and so must
eat to burn. But now, the day
reverts to type, to clear words
and the comfort of the dog we watch
unknowing, thinking we know
that she thinks this or that,
keeping her on the same lead as the mind,
casting her out before us like a reel
of line, we follow her down the lane,
ignoring what's behind;
she runs ahead, parting the birds
before her as she goes.
The waves of birds close back
the moment we have gone,
a minor wake erased, in the long
blue gaze of days—a blink.
She doesn't notice this, or so we think.

# The Love of What Is Not

*1. Cityscape*

The eye is trapped in a cul-de-sac—
the streets a half-lit box, the sky a lid.
Now and then you can hear the pop pop pop
of semi-automatics down the block. Dawn,
the waste is everywhere—the gutters run
with it, the trash turns to a black gum
in the rain and builds a silt of sewage
along the curbs. Every pile of bundled rags
breathes with a labored heave, the anonymous
rise and fall of drugged lungs; every steam vent
wears a human cover, the underground
exhales its saving heat.
                                        It feels late
in the Middle Ages, and sure enough,
there on the corner are those made mad
by God, blocking the way, branding
with their damning words the young
who pass with lowered heads
heading for the women's clinic door.
You can almost smell the burning flesh
as the words make contact, sear.
"Murderers!" one shouts, wild with need,
conviction. But of what? What moves

the zealots who rise at dawn
to arm themselves with signs—
against what foe?
What is the furnace of this heat?

              One carries, on a stick,
the crescent image, enormously enlarged,
of some creature from an underwater realm—
huge head, unformed arms, its marbled
eyes sightless, its shape not human yet,
exposed, and magnified by loss:
is this a last ditch loyalty
to what she might have been? —
the bud that never opened to the sun,
the unlived life she carries
like a fetus suspended inside
a bottle of formaldehyde
in a medical museum.

        •     •     •

This is the city we have made:
blank walls of brick, shining
towers of steel and glass, gutters
running with waste, the living
dead, and there, its sign—
a tender embryonic thing
exposed, as if the city wore
its unborn soul outside itself,
torn out and held up
to the light, huge fetus
in a hydrogen balloon,
its string cut, floating

now, above the City Hall,
into the blue, growing
smaller and smaller, shrinking
until it is no larger than
an atom of dust,
the prick
of a pin,
this
period.


## 2. E. T., I. U., and That Old-Time Religion

Up there, on the movie screen,
a strange encounter happens: the old celestial
dream, its jasper stone and gates of pearl,
lowers from the sky; with bated breath
the faithful watch this miracle occur,
and wait, eyes huge with hope.
*"I John saw the holy city, new Jerusalem, coming down*
*from God out of heaven...* **Behold, I make all things**
**new."** And so it descends, singing, a gospel
UFO, resplendent with the jeweled lights
of Revelation, yet landing like a hovercraft,
and opening its shining steel side, it
lowers a gangplank to disgorge
our saviors from the sky,
as the script implies they are to be.

But what emerges from this sci-fi craft
sent from the blue dominion of a naive faith
is a crew to break the heart—huge
fetal heads and ancient eyes, raw skin
so thin it shows the pulsing veins, and limbs
so new and delicate they are barely
flesh at all, tender lives so fresh and
vulnerable you want to stow them back
inside imagination's womb until they're ready
for the sudden light. Nothing
really happens after that. The film ends.
The red exit lights beckon.
No one can imagine what comes next.

Unless E.T., a brother to this otherworldly,
fetal crew, suggests how it must always end
when neoplasm, forming
deep within—made visible by biotech,
a ruby privacy undone—is put to the service
of that death-defying belief
that we are not
of this world, that some unseen high command
will lower through the air one day, like
a helicopter to a battlefield, and save us.

E.T. departs, riding an old idea,
diminishing out there, alien, far from the child
who spawned him, rocketed out into the cold
lightless expanse of outer space. We watch,
the helpless audience of a great commercial
success, as our innermost chance, the fresh
being of our planetary soul, its return
to itself, to the earth out of which it comes,
hurtles out and out and out, alien,
alone, towards a nowhere
we were always told
was home.

# Operations: Desert Shield, Desert Storm

1.

Who
are these two women, walking
through the great forum of the plain, walking
under the sun's blinded white eye,
under a hard, featureless sky, bright steel
without a trace of blue. Two women,
their shadows trailing them
like assassins.

What
are they speaking of,
so rapt in conversation they scarcely
seem to see the vacancy through which
they walk. One kicks reflexively at bits
of junk that litter the dry ground, raising
white spurts of dust that hover
at their feet like slavish hounds
of cloud, assiduous on the trail of
all lost things.
                    It is as if time itself
were a dry fountain, where the urn fills only
with pale ashes; where broken tablets

of illegible laws cobble the ground;
where church and court alike are built of bones,
a filigreed white latticework of chalk
through which the white sun casts
a black lace of shadows, widows' weeds;
where a small wind picks through debris,
an indigent in search of scraps; where,
in the desert of our god-drenched origins
the armies grow again, human beetles in
their masks, vague hatred with its poison
gas, the air itself a deadly trench
to these benighted boys, condemned
to fall again into the ranks
of what repeats: into the breach
once more, another city broken open like
a rotting fruit, the flies rising,
the delicate seeds exposed
to the sun, a book with a broken
spine, anything where enough
is left to name.

Antigone and Ismene,
or so we might call them,
these two women walking across this page
of history, this page that is not
a page, because no one can turn it, because
it extends and extends, the smoking cities
scattered like open lesions
to the periphery of sight, these wounds
that memory worries so they
cannot close, this sand
littered with the bodies of brothers.
These two women, whoever they might be,

have the look of those daughters
caught in the line of a self-blinded king
(a father who is also a brother)
debating again the choice
of terms—imprisoned in life, or death.
One is full of argument and heat,
an intellect who can face down a tyrant
with her tongue. The other has a downcast
face and sorrow even in the way her garments
hang, folds that hold the shadows deep
inside; though young, her soul
weighs like an ancient thing; Ismene
takes her sister's arm, to whom her life
is bound, for whose futility she feels
such a ravaged pity, and such
affection she agrees to lose
their argument, pretend to a weakness
she could never own, because she knows
the anger of Antigone must speak
although it end as an echo in a chamber
sealed in the granite hills, a tomb
whose stone is always rolled away
too late. Ismene, grieving,
lives, and walks the olive groves
alone, a lively shade for company.

Again, the dictator
in his empty boots
stalks the narrowing tunnels
of the streets, his little voice
widened by the megaphones of war,
death's echo amplified.
And then it is Ismene

recalls her sister to her side,
steels herself to animate
that shade, and lose her yet again,
if lose she must.

2.

What vicious agency of farce
recalled that ancient sister's act
of love, that wish for a brother's
burial? The stage darkens, the shadows
of the sisters merge, and deepen
to a common night:
                    the end of light
those young men, living, saw
(to think that horror stops the mind)
as the earthmovers pushed the tons of sand
up over them, and then rolled on.

And after the cheering crowds have gone
home, after the last yellow ribbon of sun
has faded in the west, where shall Ismene hide
when they open the cave where defiance
hangs, when those swaying sandals
brush her face, after they cut
the body down, where shall she turn
from all that is buried in the desert plot
made for headlines and parades,
a place too dry for even grief
Yesterday's news.
Too topical for poems.
Welcome home, this is
America, welcome home.

# *Bat Cave*

The cave looked much like any other
from a little distance but
as we approached, came almost
to its mouth, we saw its walls within
that slanted up into a dome
were beating like a wild black lung—
it was plastered and hung with
the pulsing bodies of bats, the organ
music of the body's deep
interior, alive, the sacred cave
with its ten thousand gleaming eyes
near the clustered rocks
where the sea beat with the leather
wings of its own dark waves.

Below the bat-hung, throbbing walls,
an altar stood, glittering with guano,
a stucco sculpture like a Gaudi
church, berserk
Baroque, stone translated into
flux—murk and mud and the floral
extravagance of wet sand dripped
from a giant hand, giving back
blessing, excrement—return
for the first fruits offered to the gods.

We stayed outside, superior
with fear, like tourists
peering through a door, whose hanging
beads rattle in the air from
one who disappeared into the dim
interior; we thought of the caves
of Marabar, of a writer who entered
and never quite emerged—
the caves' echoing black
emptiness a tunnel in the English
soul where he is wandering still. So
the bat cave on the Bali coast, not far
from Denpasar, holds us off, and beckons…

Standing there now, at the mouth
of the cave, this time we enter, feel
inside the flutter of those
many hearts, the radiant heat of pumping
veins, the stretch of wing on bone
like a benediction, and the familiar
faces of this many-headed god,
benevolent as night is
to the weary—the way at dark
the cave releases them all,
how they must lift like the foam
on a wave breaking, how many
they are as they enter
the starlit air, and scatter
in wild wide arcs
in search of fruit, the sweet bites
of mosquito…

while the great domes of our
own kind slide open, the eye
that watches, tracks the skies,
and the huge doors roll slowly back
on the hangars, the planes
push out their noses of steel,
their wings a bright alloy
of aluminum and death, they roar
down the runways, tear into
the night, their heavy bodies fueled
from sucking at the hidden
veins of earth; they leave a trail of fire
behind them as they scar
the air, filling the dreams
of children, sleeping—anywhere,
Chicago, Baghdad—with blood,
as the bombs drop, as the world
splits open, as the mothers
reach for their own
in the night of the falling
sky, madness in
method, nature gone
into reverse...

here, nearly unperturbed,
the bats from the sacred cave
fill the night with their calls,
high-pitched, tuned to the solid world
as eyes to the spectrum of light, gnats
to the glow of a lamp; the bats
circle, the clouds wheel,
the earth turns
pulling the dome of stars

among the spinning trees, blurring
the sweet globes of fruit, shaped
exactly to desire—dizzy, we swing
back to the cave on our stiff dark
wings, the sweet juice of papaya
drying on our jaws, home
to the cave, to attach ourselves
back to the pulsing dome, until,
hanging there, sated and sleepy,
we can see what was once our world
upside down as it is
and wonder whose altars
those are, white,
encrusted with shit.

**two**

*Variations on the*
*Ides of March*

# The Bird in the Laurel's Song

"How long have I been here? I can't recall
how many suns have risen and withdrawn
since I came down to this branch to rest.

"How strange it felt at first, warm
under my feet, and when I landed here
and clamped my claws around its bark
I could have sworn I heard a moan. Is this
the work of men, I wondered then,
who like to decoy us with images of wood
we take for friend, then lie in wait for us, armed,
their arrows tipped with our own feathers.
Yet this was opposite of that—a tree that feels
like wood, an ordinary laurel, leaves a polished
green, but with a pulse inside, I swear,
the engine of a heart like mine; and something
not quite planted in its stance, the way it swayed
and seemed to reach out toward me as I passed.
And so I stopped, and sat.
                              But I'm uneasy
now, the forest ways are broken here,
some sadness haunts this tree
that I fear, mortally, to sound. Nor can I sing
when these leaves rustle in the air
around my perch, and breathe and whisper

in my ear, and speak of what I cannot
bear, nor compass with my airborne
mind—some deep attachment to the ground
whose price is to be rooted there; it makes
my wings ache with the thought, and
I must fly away from here, but yet am held
in dappled light like a net of lace
that will not let me go. O gods,
if you can break the spell that holds us
both together in this glade, then I will
stay with what it is within that suffers here."

      The river stirred in a passing wind, and the sun,
      stretched out on its back, moved
      in a shiver of gold, and a woman appeared
      by the river's bank, looked around
      as if awakened from a dream, a little dazed.
      She reached down to pick the book up
      that had fallen at her side, and some flowers
      she had gathered in a nearby field. Then,
      following the river bank, she wandered off,
      singing to herself.

      "But it was I who sang,
though I look out through her eyes;
it is I whom the gods hear, I who laid down
my wings, and nested here out of love."

# Afterwards

"…mind was steadfast as before;
so wept they as they were penned up."
—*Odyssey*, 10.240–41

We are back now—standing, dazed in the mud,
no fallen bristles around our feet, no
visible sign of what we were. O gods!
And him, our leader, standing there grinning—
the agent, so he thinks, of our salvation.
He, who brought us here, who has not been
what we have been—down in those trenches,
lost in a storm of mud, the stench of our own
excrement, the air we were forced to breathe—
swine in those ditches, and food for swine.

After the battles, the R & R; after the mud, brothels;
after the blood, swine. Oh, remember the music
that roused us so, the glory we were going for,
our leaders standing on the bow, a splendor
in their uniforms, gold on their shoulders, a sprawl
of gold uncoiling on the visors of their caps,
only their eyes in shadow. We were the eagle's
spawn, the troops of rosy-fingered dawn;
everything hummed with light, sun glinting
on bronze—there was nothing we couldn't defend.

And after all, were we still men, penned there
in the shape of what was vile? Our minds
were steadfast as before; that was the horror—
we were, and were not, men, condemned
to stay aware, who could not free ourselves of filth,
the ditch to which enchantment led. Would that we
had loved him less, believed our senses more—
he of the devious ways who knew too well
our steadfast minds, and led us to the pens,
then vanished as the gate swung shut.

Night now, he is telling stories again, wrapping
more innocents around his honeyed tongue—
as he took us to the lotus fields, and sold us
dreams, but never inhaled that powder.
And tied to the mast, his ears immune,
did he laugh as our brothers threw themselves
into the waves' dark troughs? Night now;
in its cover we will drag him from the court's
adoring gaze and cast him to the mob
waiting in the mud, swine at the palace gate.

# How to Get in the Best Magazines

Preferred:
tired little poems, taut,
world-weary, properly bored
with it all, though still a bit awed
by atrocity, choosy
among the data, the minutiae
in which we live—hikers
caught in a biting swarm of blackflies.
Look for the few words, the image
to catch, exactly, ennui; the odd bone
of a finger sticking through the sod
of the freshly laid lawn, something
small, dry and horrible
to prod us, to stick in the craw
for a moment—a brief sign
of remembrance
between the ads for Neiman Marcus
and the Inn with exclusive arrangements,
its own private bay and a dock.

Produce, please, a poem that will fit
in a slot between fiction and furs, one
to go down like a silky martini,
chilled from its small bout with the ice,
leaving only the green globe of olive,
tiny and gone in a bite, its acid tang
lingering around the pit, small
and hard in your mouth—
the one bit of grit
is what's wanted, that pearl
beyond price: there
is the minimal poem, the absolute
disappointment, the one
you will want
to submit.

If, sadly, you slipped, inserted a bird,
loud on the sill in its lush spray of feathers,
or a scurry of feet in a bed of heartsease,
a green as layered and dense as a Balinese
screen, a light air, angelic tread
of sunlight on the water, a climate
of friends, an afternoon's sufficiency
among so many summers—
rejection must follow,
as surely as suburbs
in the wake of the cities.

If we, who have cost the world so much
additional suffering, who are so heedless
in plunder,
               if we could not, this afternoon
or some other, be happy, replete,
or harvest at least
some richness out of the native
air;
        if we can only perfect
the thin arts of unhappiness,
the tongue's anorexia
playing its riff in the hollow
horn of plenty, the world a mere
annex to the mortgaged house
of our discontent,
                         then
it is time to write
the acceptable poem—
ice and glass, with its splinter
of bone, its pit
of an olive,
the dregs
of the cup of abundance,
useless spill of gold
from the thresher, the dust
of it filling the sunlight, the chum
broadcast on the black waters
and the fish
    —the beautiful, ravenous fish—
refusing to rise.

# The Muse

There she was, for centuries, the big
broad with the luscious tits, the secret
smile, a toga of translucent silk, cool
hand on the shoulder of the suffering
poet—the tease who made him
squeeze those great words out. He
was the mirror *and* the lamp, she the torch
who burned with the blue butane of a pure
refusal, too good for mortal use; her breath
was cold as mountain streams, the chill
of the eternal—no hint of plaque
or any odor of decay. Ethereal as hell,
a spirit in chiffon, the mystery is
how she had got so rounded in the butt
and all her better parts as soft as butter,
why such a wraith should be so ample,
what her endowments had to do
with that for which she set example—
all this was surely Mystery, oh that elusive
object of desire, that "untouch'd bride
of quietness," that plump poetic dish
who lived on air but looked
as if she dined on pasta.

Basta!
A pox on the great Lacan,
who writes with his eraser, on all poetic
Graces, mute and pensive, concave exactly
where he is most extensive—oh look
what she has *not* that he has got,
a thing I'm too polite to mention
except to say it rhymes with Venus,
it was the Latin word for tail;
its root, therefore, is *not* the same as pen,
which comes from the word for feather.

But enough of these fine distinctions.
What a great tradition was born when
Alexander whipped his penknife out, cut
the knot she carefully had tied, leaped
on his mount, a perfect straddle
and let the crotch decide
who was the horse and who was the rider,
who was the muse and who
the writer.

# *Out of the Hellespont*

THE OLD STORY: When a jealous wrangle threatened
the life of her children, Phrixus and Helle, the cloud-
goddess Nephele transported them through the air on
a golden-fleeced ram. But during the escape, Helle fell
from the back of the cloud-borne sheep into the sea
below, which afterwards bore her name. When Phrixus
reached safety, he offered up the ram, hanging its gold-
en fleece on a tree guarded by a sleepless dragon, an
unintentional goad to future heroes, Jason and his Arg-
onauts. Later, through offense to Zeus, each firstborn
male in the line of Phrixus was marked for ritual sacri-
fice to the god—unless he could escape in time.

I.

Off the map, out there,
as centuries recede like shores
from a departing ship, she swims
in the strait that bears her name,
in that sweet blue that darkens
as you dive, she feels the waves slide
cool along her flanks
and sees the light through
waving fronds with ornamental eyes,
the fins and tentacles of swirling
sea, unlike the empty air
through which she fell, her call
like a smoke trail, fading…
already gone before
the waves closed
like a hand, around her.

Her brother rode the flying ram
with the fleece of gold, to port—
killed it, skinned it, hung its bright
wool on a tree, shorn as St. Catherine's
blond curls in the relic box
by her grinning skull
with its gossamer bridal veil.
He left a serpent to guard
the golden fleece, went off to rule, to war,
to keep the line alive, the line
of males for sacrifice. Should she have
clung to him, gone along for the ride,
back to the butcher's work of history,
back to breed for the infantry?
Can she be blamed for letting go,
for languid days spent in the waves
where sight turned blue, the coral hummed,
and water wove with light as in a dream?


2.

Of late, a strange wind blew
from off the land—a shrill voice
like an anxious mother's
as light begins to fail,
calling her child in. The sea
itself was sick, a poison
seemed to spread through its wine-
dark veins; all sanctuary gone,
she knew she'd have to break
the surface tension, climb
the stones that line the broken
borders of their worlds.

. . .

Now, rising from the waves,
she is no Aphrodite, foam born,
with beauty's marble torso, its pensive
living head. As tides withdraw,
sweep out the morning shells in evening's
ebb; as the crest of each wave hangs
a moment in the air before
it falls, before the next one
rising, builds; as foam will
sign the margins in a white and
cursive hand, no sooner written than,
in a million bubbles bursting,
the sand goes blank again—
so foam-made figures fade
like names from water-logged maps,
new footprints mark the sand:
suspended for a moment
like a figure just emerging
from a myth, wet with life,
she reaches for a towel
to wipe her salt-stung eyes
and wrap herself against
the air, its unaccustomed chill.

# Leda's Handmaiden

I was Leda's intimate, and slave,
born, as I was, on the losing side,
where the mind grows agile,
and the heart's true tongue
learns to put on fable for disguise.
Take, for example, the swan—
it came to me as we shook
the pillows out and a few white feathers
flew. How she laughed when I spoke
the thought aloud—how the god
would rape her in the swan's white shape
with the winged ease of miracle,
but big, believable: the serpent's neck,
the malign eye, the yellow webs
of its feet pinning her arms,
the terrible beak—Zeus,
a perfect cover for a king too old for love
in whom the dry seed rattled like a gourd.
Now I look back, I think perhaps
the fabrication a mistake—fuel to set
the bright sparks of desire ablaze,
a whetstone to ambition's
extra axe-bright edge.

Though everything can be forgotten
(or so sunk in memory's swamp
that the shape to which emotion clings
is lost), consequence goes on,
the unexpected spawn of our exploits,
and even of our lies—like Leda's pair
of girls, the pawns of fame,
her joy of them left out like babies
for the pigs to eat. Her boys, gold stars
hung in a mother's pane. Murder and war,
and the animal roar of a city
put to the torch—born from those nights
of love. I think of his tread
on the porch, the dust of his boots
on her floor, the thick Persian lamb
of his hair. How afterwards
Leda and I gave rumor wings, shaking
swansdown on her bed, airing out
the sweet male smell of sperm,
for the seed of gods is
odorless, like light.

It was I who led him to her room
and I who told the story
that the lyre takes
from court to court, and I who had him
first, and after, too, for he was
mine—the sons he got of me, oh…
two were drowned at sea, two died
at the walls of Troy, one lives
but is not whole. Our daughters,
practiced in the arts of grief, are
widows all. Cold beds, moth-eaten coats
hung on history's hook, a name
that flutters like a sleeve.
And the children left behind—
for them I fill the vacancy
with tales, to guide the plow
that furrows memory, the gift
of a lady's slave, poured
into the ear of a war-blinded son
who is a comfort to my age,
that one—because he loves
the tales I tell, because
he sings them in a cadence
that would crack a stone
god's heart; at night
when sleep despises me,
I write them down,
I sign the name
we share.

# *Ambition*

I didn't always think Penelope
a fool. We used to play together
when we were girls, and she could
outswim anyone, and on a dare would
grab a dolphin's fin and ride the wind
across the island's bay, or shinny up
a tree and swing from the highest branch
as if the gods had not invented
fear. I was more cautious by far,
more prone to seeing things
before wind blew the smoke away—I'd see
the bones before the fire was out,
the blood before the blow was struck,
the storm when it was still a mile
out. But that is like me, isn't
it, to bring the tale around, back
to myself? It is Penelope I meant
to tell you more about, and how she
changed when she met him, the wily
one, Odysseus, my callow brother.
For I am Nobody's sister, the name
he took to trick the bullies, before
he could afford his own. His fame
is now on every tongue, well known

to the widows of Ithaca, a curse
in the mouths of the women
he ordered hung—his concubines
who lay with other men the twenty
years when he was gone. Lord
of Ithaca, bowlegged, strutting
about the town, telling everyone
tales, Mr. Adventurer, the brilliant
leader who came home alone—
his ships sunk, his men
bones for the sea to rattle.

Penelope was wildest of us all,
her mind as agile as an ibex
on a mountain wall, skipping
from one outrageous notion to
the next, never slipping or losing
her footing. Quick to anger, she was
always sorry after. A fire
seemed to flicker over her; it caught
when her first blood came. A woman's
first blood is her bright signature
of life; a man's first blood is wound—
his own, another's, blood shed
in war, or torn from a girl
he forces, or the deer he pins
with arrows to the earth. So her desire
for him brought fear into her heart, as Kore
picks each spring those flowers
whose roots, when pulled, will rouse up
Hell. She who would be ruled by nobody
became his fool.
                    My brother. As a boy
he had been sent to study war and numbers

somewhere far across the sea, the place
where sun arises, gold and yawning, from his couch
each dawn. And bright as a god returning
he must have seemed to her, for she,
my wild friend, gazed at him—something
in her blazed, then seemed to freeze. She turned
the way the goat's milk turns
to cheese—she seemed
to thicken and grow solid; she left
her bright self in the sun
of memory; she wanted
nothing but to hover in his shade.

And how he loved it, liar brother,
that great Nobody he pretended, never
where he said he'd be, and nothing
but a chaser after women—
he must have slept with everyone
he saw once he had tired
of having her. And when her belly
swelled with Telemachus, he was off
to war; his son grew up without him,
while she became his living monument,
his name carved in the deep grooves
of her brain. The endless shroud she wove
was never finished; she didn't have to
struggle anymore—he was her great
excuse: frame, thread and pattern.

No use my hoping to unravel
what she had herself
so seamlessly created, the rack
of her clattering loom.
                    For she, who had
not feared the cracking of the branches
when she'd swung out dangling in the air, and she
who'd crammed the darkening mulberries in
her mouth till it was crimson, outdanced the stars
and washed the moon down in the brimming
cups of wine, and led us up the hills in darkness
to the Mysteries where she whirled
until she seemed the foam that lashes heaven
on a wave—she
was broken by the chance
encounter with a man so empty
she could sit for twenty years, the perfect
husk of the cicada, and all she was
flown out into the distance, into him.


                    Well, I will spoil his story,
liar brother, tale spinner. Our other brother
I loved well, and truly—he was my friend,
whose name was folded in the flames
that took him. We poured so many treasures
on it, his pyre lit the skies
for days. Had he lived to be the one
to rule the island, perhaps it
might have gone another way.
And how I wished Penelope
had chosen wisely. But this is
how it goes—she chose mirage, the sheen
of distance, a shield's flash, wave foam struck by sun.
So now our island's poor, our women bitter, the children rootless,

there is this tiresome couple—old Odysseus
bragging of his exploits, stony Penelope
dragging through the halls, and me,
Nobody's sister, who watched
and could change nothing

but all the time was
plotting
another story
in which our better brother
lives, in which Penelope
keeps her wild wits
about her, I finally get the part
I wanted—it is my
fingers on the lyre, Apollo's
whore, I who tore the hearts
of Ithaca, as cloth is torn
for tourniquets
to staunch the pouring blood;
my song that called the moon
to wrap the sea back sweet around
the island, to make the marble pebbles chuckle
on the beach each time a wave receded;
my song that made them
love the orchards of abundant olive,
the laden vines of peace, and
made them
hate the dogs of glory
and laugh
with the gods' own laughter
catching Ares
in bed with Aphrodite—
stupid beauty, dazed and
drunken war.

# The Lament of the Valkyrie

Always the fair extensions of his will,
we'd had no thought but him—his chill
our misty climate, the air we breathed;
a gloomy god, full of dark forebodings, empty
of regrets. At his feet, a pair of silver wolves;
ravens for epaulettes; and war for sport.

I forget the day it began to sicken me,
notwithstanding the sweet rewards
of such a role, its bright celebrity;
and not just me, the others too,
began to hate this lottery—
the choosing of the slain.

When did the armor's weight seem more than flesh
could bear—the silver sheen we'd polished
to a rival shine with moon, so when we rode,
the battlefield's red flares played over our steel skins
in jagged tints of fire, the Aurora Borealis
of the northern skies, the glorious shimmer of war?

Was it the day when, swooping in, collecting heroes
for the gods to set like bloody dolls
along the trestle tables in Valhalla's deathless
halls, our horses suddenly reared, refused
to answer to the rein, their nostrils
wide, indignant, at the smell?

Was it then we first looked down and saw
that blighted spring, as if awakened from a mead-
soaked dream, what rain uncovered at our feet,
half-mired in mud—mere boys, eighteen
or less, oozing the blood, the brains, the seed
meant to quicken life again?

And saw, as if our eyes were newly made,
how the mud matted their hair to the same dull slate
as their eyes, cold embers on which the breath
of myth could blow, to kingdom come
or Götterdämmerung, and never
bring the least glow back to those dead eyes.

So we dismounted, led our anxious horses
from the field, put down our shields, and knelt
to lift the helmets from our heads, to shed
the iron weight; the clamor of our falling armor
was like the wreck of anthems; we felt
blood stir, flow back to our stiff limbs.

Our swords we kept, withdrew into the room
whose darkened corner held the loom
where we had learned the trick of weaving
murder into art; and there, in all that dusk,
we cut "the crimson web of war"
and then, our own bright plaited hair

that once had flown among the banners
luring innocence to war—outdoors
at the field's edge, shorn as winter's
lambs, we left insignias of braided gold
already beginning to darken and sink
in the merciful mud of spring.

And since it happened as I've said
(though memory too grows dark and blurs
until I can't be sure which field it was, or year)—

from ruined Valhalla's walls, why do I hear
wolves howl, the beat of raven wings,
the same old trumpet call?

# *After the Snow Queen*
# *Lost Her Charm*

It seemed important once, the halls of snow
that called, beckoning the boy-self
kept carefully in the attic flat next door
across the water-gutter garden
from your room, where you would play,
press hot pennies to the icy glass
and make a frosted circle for the eye
to fill with its blue dreaming
iris sky, gazing out
for endless centuries of childhood.

The fallen mirror, the first encounter
with the deconstructing demons
of the mind, detached, who made all beauty
seem a lie, the greenest hills mere
spinach to the disenchanted eye, until,
lifting that disabling mirror
one notch too high, and filling it with
seedy angels, far gone in moult, they lost
their grip and dropped their glittering
device—its mocking splinters sowed
a bitter wind: postmodern
born before its time,
lordly culture's bastard son.

Those splinters caught the eye,
the heart, of that boy Kay, the friend
in the high facing room of childhood,
free of all adults except
Grandmother, generic, gray time's
familiar, sad witness to the way
the splinters entered him,
how he grew mocking in his gaze,
became nay-sayer, underminer;
pulled the petals off the rose
(she loves, she loves me not)
to prove love cannot stay.

And how you felt it too, the pull
of the beautiful royal woman all
in white, a crystal countenance,
a coat of fur that like a snowdrift
drew you in, the soft and sleep-
inducing cold that felt like care,
the kind of mothering that was all
pretense, decor, flowers in a vase,
and to submit to her embrace was
to be changed—encased,
an irritating bit of dirt
like something in the eye that blurs
the world with tears and hurt,
but in the cool embrace of beauty's shell,
that mollusk urn would slowly
pour its molten silk around your soul
until you were a perfect pearl,
a fly in amber, a crystal with its
small, imperfect speck that, seen
up very close, looked like an open
mouth, shaped by a wordless howl.

These fears we understood; they
seemed important then, those gorgeous
queens who beckoned through the frosted
glass, whose swan-drawn sleighs were
hitched to every sumptuous winter cloud.
But it was Kay they always took away,
convenient almost-brother, staring
out the window on the other side, cold
mind brooding in its exile on the sill,
the boy the Queen's sled always towed
to the chiming crystal world of perfect
things, the blizzard's eye, ice chamber
where a melody, once played, hangs still,
echoes forever fading in the frozen air.

So we, the Gerdas of the dream, set out,
casting our red shoes off, coasting
the water's back, the current
grabbing the canoe, the barefoot
trip begun, attractions littering
the way, the floral fantasies
permitted girls—dear old ladies
with their gardens, Lotus-Eaters
of the rosy-colored glass, eternal
spring, the petals soft as Kleenex,
roses rising from our tears, and
from the mists, what else, a palace
suddenly unveiled, whose Prince and
Princess found our case appealing,
our motives pure, and loaned
their gilded carriage, a little horse,
a muff of fur, and boots.

Thus all was well, our wardrobe growing,
virtue constantly accruing, when
the story took a turn and entered woods,
dark woods—the scalp begins to crawl
just to remember—the worst part,
where we begged our mother
to read faster, faster, to escape
the dark, the band of robbers, for whom
the gold in which our innocence was set
was lure; the little robber girl,
whose filth and cunning ways upset
the flower cart in which our minds
had traveled: the air was dank, and fear
was a skinny wolf who slunk along beside us
in the shadows. The robbers' lair:
women with beards, and knives,
a biting daughter who sunk her teeth
into her drunken mother—the little robber
girl who wanted you to sleep beside her,
her long blade at her side, and at
your throat, if you should cross her. Yet
in the tale, it's she who sets you free,
and, with you, the reindeer she had loved
to torture; she sets you riding
on its back, the shimmer of the Northern Lights
caught on the candlelabra of its antlers—
to where the cold center of the story
sits, a diamond the size of a glacier
lit by the white of the moon.

But hope returns with heat—the hearth
of the Finn woman where the last advice
was given; then Gerda's own warm breath
formed friendly legions in the frigid
air who broke the brittle
snowflake guard at the Snow Queen's
crystal gate. At last: the denouement—
in which the snowdrift castle with
its frozen lake of splintered mind
is opened to the heart, and Kay,
all but gone in blue transparencies,
is warmed by Gerda's tears,
and the two escape together from
the Hall of Reason and the Snow
Queen's spell, a lovely meltdown.

And they head home to bathe in Grandma's
smile, two heads together bent
over one Book, one Rose—and now,
when all of this seems fly-specked
by the years, a Northern fable for good
children: the girl all hearth and
spunk, the boy all numbers, numbness,
gibes; the two not really one
but two, and side by side forever,
requiring one another, and the Snow Queen
shrunk to a cut-glass figurine…yet
something stuck in memory's craw,
like the hook the hunter wraps in fat
for the bear to swallow—

it takes hold later,
the part you hated as a child: the dirty
lair, the little robber girl, last seen
on her stolen horse, a scarlet cap on her head
and pistols in her belt: "it was
the little robber girl, who was tired
of being at home," who rode off
into the world while we succumbed
to the story's end, drawn back to the town with
its tell-tale towers, the gardens bursting into
flower...

       and back in the wood we were led
to forget, birds of mottled black and white
move as if on ratchets on the bark,
each head a scarlet cap,
they hammer a furious song—the fallen
hammer of Thor, broken
music everywhere, driving
a thousand beaks,
a chorus growing louder
as the darkening woods become
the anvil of
the oldest gods
sharpening their knives.

# "...as soft and as pink as a nursery..."

This is the good child
in his bed. Beside him, his mother
with her sweet pink face, her nice
manners, her extremely well-manicured
fingers, her strange desire to have him
perfectly untouched, so that her hands
are always running over him,
pushing his hair back and exposing
his hot, gleaming face, wiping
his nose with the edge
of her tissue, picking
at things on his clothes: little bits
of thread, dust, food, lint
of a world that clings to him
almost lovingly—these she assiduously removes
as if she were his valet
grooming him for a starring role, the curtain
about to go up, and only her between him
and the humiliating abyss
of some unforgivable gaffe,
the laughter of strangers...

this is the good mother
who, as the light fades to mauve
and the corners begin to fill with distended
shadows, reads him stories full of vengeful,
hairy, bad-tempered and evil-smelling
monsters, huge as Hindenbergs, engorged
with centuries of crimes imagined
in millions of nurseries, waxing
in the growing dark of bedtime; genies
festering with long imprisonment—planning
at first, gold and deep gratitude
to their rescuers; later, after years
in the jar, beginning to plot
the gifts that bring ruin; finally,
bloated with a rage
so murderous, so purely tabloid
and horribly true, that to lift out the cork
were to loose Pandora's swarm of evils
without a hope to flutter after...

the little boy can do nothing but watch
as these colossal figures fill the little space
that is his room, their thick legs rising
like the trunks of redwoods, their distant
shoulders looming like cliffs, their necks
periscopes peering into the black intangible
sky, from where he hears, booming,
the arrogant thunder of their laughter
so that even the stars are shaken
as if the night were a thick black mass
of icy gelatin in which the stars
were caught, shivering and burning...

he draws himself up tight under the quilt,
a still, small mound that watches
round-eyed as the monsters pour
from the pink heart-shaped mouth
of his mother, who now and then smiles sweetly,
calls him her little man, her bug, her pet,
and fiddles with the button at her neck.

# The Secret Garden

The way you see it first is through
the keyhole, that aperture with hips,
and one you have to crouch down low
in front of, and squint to get a look
inside. A green space glows, oh it is
pretty, as aqueous as an aquarium,
where slender shapes, finned and neon-
spotted, glide beside your eyes, and press
their tiny noses to your glasses. Lean
closer, the keyhole holds the Mystery, until
of course, a key's inserted and spoils
the view. Meanwhile, the green invites you:
rosehips, clinging vines, the shy nasturtium,
grapes by the pound, diminutive white lilies
of the valley, pussy willows; in the shade,
moss, moss on every stone, moss crawling
the walls, moss over roots, soft, smothering
moss—underneath it all: a million worms,
brown, segmented, one end like the other,
a poem that ends with its opening line.

When it rains in the secret garden,
the worms come out and sport; they push
their wet way through the parting
particles of soil, they slip through mulch
and lift their small snub noses, faces
empty of expression as a toe, and lo,
they dance among the fallen petals, cavort
in the brackish puddles, splash and writhe
until the garden is alive with coils
and coils of shining brown (a python
if you think of them together)—until
the earth itself is pure Medusa, lost
head of blue spinning through the vacant
cosmos, its crust a fume of writhing
serpents... and that, dear Jack,
is what is in the secret garden:
you are invited to come in for tea. But
bring your own cup and a folding chair,
and do wear rubbers, as there is danger
of infection, and we should hate
to think the worms could get you
before we're through with tea.

# Last Words

*Blind Oedipus*
*is old, death sits*
*at his side, its cold breath*
*on his hand. If you lean close,*
*you can hear him speak:*


"Cursed with words, yet still
   they are my eyes, and what I say
      I see: old men
who put their sons on distant hills
 to die, and calling it god's will,
those armies of the young are led
    to think the enemy
  is somewhere over there
and so are spared the messenger's
arrival with the news:    the twisted root,
       the lame foot—your father's legacy
      to you, your mother dreaming
      the king's dream, the oracle mouthing
      his desires,
          the rain dark
as we begin, like statues
made of earth, to melt back into mud,

eyes pouring water, faces streaked
and losing shape, returning to earth—
      like the terra-cotta army
      buried in the tomb
      of the Emperor Qin, but this time
      no beautiful figures to dig up,
      no one to comment on the exquisite realism,
      how each face is faithful
      to its original, the way each costume
      shows the rank, how the handsome horses
      flank imperial pride—only
one common mud, earth closing
over its own eyes…

we, who would give dumb matter
voice, and to inherent numbers bring
an intricate and abstract mirror, and span
the distance between stars with the silver
strands of mind, and link all difference
in the shimmering bridge
of imagery, and with blind molecules
grow eyes and hands that, phototropic,
grope their way to light,
pull all creation in our wake
into the brilliant day—and yet
as twins will hatch from the selfsame egg,
awareness split between its joys
and horror at the short term set to them,
the quick return
of dark, the mind fell under
the spell of death, which took
no end of forms:

             a lost shoe, a blighted hope, a misplaced
         name, the slightest hint of disagreement
from a subordinate, a woman
         out of reach, the sight of a young
                 son growing strong
could bring on rage, the blood
wash in the eyes, the red letter
days of war, the bellow
                 of a dying animal—
         Mud, I say, and mud, I see,
         all dark, I say, from so much
         light, from such abundant
         vision as I had, such
         abomination, such
         continual night."


*If you wish, you may close*
*his eyes now, and close*
*the quote, put*
*the double marks,*
*like the bite of a small animal,*
*there, on the white page.*

# Fears about the Moon

The silk strands tangle in the hands

*What if the tide went out and did not return?*

the knots are everywhere, the silk too fine,
the hands too tense... up there above the strand
of beach, the silver threads of water fall,
cataracts on the rock's sheer face
where the thin breath of mist hovers
like fine dust from a lathe
where precious metals once were worked,
the bench is empty now, the smith fled, what remains
is a fine scrim of gold dust in the air, silver
in the hair, the world seen through a dimming haze
of failed alchemy—the rotten gold fruit
of myth: apple, fig, the split skin
of banana on which ants swarm
like stars

*What if the tide refused and the sea kept going out?*

So the hands fall idle, lie open
as flowers dropped in the lap, or palm fronds
blown from the tree, left absent on the sand,
slowly turning brown
in the sun's noncommittal light
that brings the seed up green or takes
the color back from everything
detached

> *And what if the waves should not turn back? What if*
> *the moon let go, merely a rind in the sky*
> *that day will fade to a hint of cloud, a name*
> *that once dragged even*
> *the sea behind it, but now*
> *brings nothing to mind*

And the empty hand stirs, scoops up
sand, mother-of-pearl ground down
too fine to recognize; only the shine, that odd sparkle
when light plays on the precious little that is
left, reminds us of what breathed inside— even in stone
a pulse, a mouth, opened and shut with tidal feasts

> *But what if the tide should cease?*

Now the hand, its tan curve holding sand, opens
slowly—as a flower would if we could stay, be still
enough to see—the hand opens, the fingers slowly spreading
like the pinions of a bird in flight, the palm
fronds in the trees above begin
to stir the air like oars of tattered sail,
the sand begins to slide, a run of grains
through the outspread hand
to the beach below, though a few grains
cling to the palm's creased skin
where the lifeline fades into other lines
so imperceptibly it can't be read.
The breeze picks up the fringes
on the fallen fronds that lie along the sand,
and makes a little stir, as wind
across a battlefield flutters the rags of the dead
and the moon flies its small white flag

>        *Far out at sea the tide turns with a curse, as if*
>        *a sleeper had been roused, quite suddenly, from sleep;*
>        *begins its slow, almost reluctant roll*
>        *toward shore, pushing the tons of sand up the steep*
>        *incline toward the beach, where, among the palms,*
>        *Earth pulls the moon behind it as it turns;*
>        *the crescent, setting in the early dark*
>        *like a hook in the horizon's*
>        *lip, drags, as on an unseen line of silk,*
>        *the vast and listless tides*

# *Those Who Come After*

will never say of us:
*what wonderful myths they had.*
There will never rise, dripping, from our midst
figures whose wings open, dry in the sun,
completed by being
more us than ourselves; what we leave
is all that can be
dredged up from wrecked harbors—
history's debris. So
in the end, it is not the beautiful figures
draped in the white silk togas of dream
nor the muscular thoughts stalking the peaks
in the golden proportions of Greece
with the lightning clenched in their fists,
nor the animal-gods with the eyes of hawks
and the delicate fingers of girls,
no, only what broke in our hands
when our voyages—like the stick in the paw
of the monkey, extending the grasp—
ended in the slow grip
of possession, as a continent's shore is
slowly swallowed by sea, making an infinite
coastline, the in and out of an edge
endlessly nibbled and gnawed. That

is the line we leave behind us,
the infinity of rat-tooth,
the posterity of loss...

But when they say of us
what we have done, perhaps they will speak
kindly of those who, near the century's
end, pried open the hand;
of the way the wind lifted the lovely
gray spirals of ash, until our hands
were empty as a cloudless sky,
empty as altars whose offerings
had been acceptable; perhaps they will
say that there were those
who took down the harps
hung in the sorrowing trees, having lost
the taste for conquest or revenge,
and made a song
that rose in the air
as smoke rises—
at first a line, and then,
slow eddies, the spirals
endless, unwinding
the sky's blue
spool.

**three**   *Vistas*

This landscape has absorbed the histories
and cultures of all nations, leaving us with a
nature rather than a history, a vista rather than
a scripture.

—Eric Leed, overheard at Jimmy's, Sept. 12, 1988

Slower. Silence. We are nearing Triangle.
Now the shock of the skeleton loft
unfolds the tall wall of wailing till
Heaven cracks and tatters, blesses us with rain.

—Chris Llewellyn, from *Fragments from the Fire*

# Generic Vision, 1991

A huge figure drags a body, riddled
    with wounds, across a landscape.
                         The figure
is many stories tall, a colossus,
but migrant; its westward path is a meridian
that spans the globe. The body it drags behind
it, miles long, bumps along the ground, snags
at times on outcroppings of rock, has to be
edged over, lifted off; sometimes it disappears
in water when the figure crosses rivers,
then shears the muddy banks as it is raised,
leaving a slash where nothing grows; smears
    the earth as it is dragged along, its trail
        bright as the red tail of a kite
                wavering across a darkening sky, a track
                        endless as the wound that feeds it,
                                an inexhaustible supply, thick black
                            fluid from a hidden source, staining
                    the terrain it passes over; crushing
              towns and villages, flattening forests,
      rocks becoming gravel in its wake—
its pressure is immense, it
gouges the soft earth into
canyons, pulls the hills
down to the level of the sea.

The figure
who drags the body is faceless, ponderous
as stone, though its mobility argues for
the flesh, and from it something rises
like a moan, a cry
muffled by the absence
of a mouth. The bleeding load
it drags is shrouded, wrapped in
multicolored cloths and rags resembling
faded flags, torn and streaked
by constant passage.
　　　　　The figure
moves against the turning motion
　　of the Earth, its speed exactly timed
　　　　to the planet's revolution, so that the sun
　　　　　　stays fixed above it in perpetual
　　　　　　　noon; the figure casts no shadow, walking
　　　　its treadmill way, the black blood
　　gleaming in the light that goes on
searing as the days slide into years,
　　the years to centuries, and the millennium,
　　　　winding down, spirals slowly through
　　　　　the chute of time, the empty channel
　　　　　　we have made of it, like a worm
　　　　　that leaves the hollow of its tunnels
　　　　as the scripture of its path. Just so,
　　the figure walks, the planet
　　　　slowly spins the other way, the body
　　　　　marks the road in blood; the figure
　　　　　　walks, the planet turns, the sun,
　　　　　　　through the broken ozone, burns.

# Atget's Gardens

"As I am now seventy years of age and without heirs or
progeny of any kind, I am extremely anxious about this
collection of plates."

—Eugène Atget in a letter, Nov. 12, 1920

Was it always a dream   then?

the fallen leaves   the stairs
that lead nowhere   the players
flown     plates in a drawer
was anyone *ever*  there?

nothing lives here but the light

it inhabits the place   hovers in
the groves of trees   inviting the eye
away from what it sees   as if
just behind the stairs   water
lapped a wall   and at the landing
stage   a boat were being untied
about to push away on the dark
water   just beyond your gaze
its opaque shadows thick
as the impasto of a dream
you can't remember
when you wake—

these bloodless scenes   all
color drained   even
memory has withdrawn

leaving only this one odd man

dragging his camera from one
beautiful emptiness to another
one space within the next
like Chinese boxes   they vanish
down the funnel of the camera's
lens, and then into the eye
of the man   who always waits
for what he can't recall   and wonders
what it was he lost

perhaps no one

ever entered here   the light
suffusing everything may only
seem departure's glow
unless it is the light
the dying sometimes see
when   like Atget   they face
away   though the quiet is huge
we barely hear
the water lap and lap against
the pier   the chuckle of loose
stones   the dry rustle of
the half-lit leaves
the hush of a prow
cleaving
water

# Demolition

Once, cool in silk whose rich hem slid
with the easy flow of water over stone,
we walked in the gardens of China,
calm imperium of green, and it was jade
in its composure—only wind chimes, in a distance
more remote than any dream, shivered
the imperturbable air, wrinkled
a moment the smooth skin
of the pool with its single huge
carp, the deep orange of mandarin, ponderous
as a fish of brass, floating,
as a world hangs in space, suspended
in the nets of invisible laws.
A lily pad of heavy leather rested
lightly there, its ivory blossom open—
a mouth of white silk tongues
to drink the silence in. Above, one cloud
drifted by like a reflection of the flower
in heaven's mirror, and a kite
in the shape of a carp; below,
one arched bridge,
doubled in the pond
made a perfect
ring of Chinese red.

When the first drop fell, the image
shook, then shattered into jagged shards
of red that shuddered on the dark
face of the water; then
the bridge itself was rising
toward the sky—it held its shape
a held breath fraction of a second
before it went to pieces
in the air. It felt as if the eye were
shattered with it; we could no longer tell
the bits that shivered as they tore
apart from one another in the air
from the red reflections
in the agitated water, frantic as a school
hit by the detonation
of a bomb, the sudden scatter
of the stunned, who, dead
a moment later, float up
to the surface, bloated
bodies at the mercy
of the current,
carried
on the dragon's
back, downstream
to where the river opens
like a fan; there we wait
to gather in our baskets
what we can—the gleaming scales
of sunlight on the water, the shadows
of our reaching hands.

# What Was Left Over

—for Sujata Bhatt

1.

As you said, Sujata, it was not
mentioned, was kept out
of the story, out of the elaborate ritual
of parting and redemption, the gorgeous
sanction of sacrifice—that plunge
into the heart of fire, the drugged victim
or the fear-crazed hero, the scattered
entrails of power, of belief—
but there, you described it, how the elephants
gather, how they circle, and see it; how they
see it and mourn: the torn carcass
with the head taken for the trophy room
of the gods; the stumps where a tusk
or a forest once grew;

      the priest wiping clean
the blood of a lean season from the ritual
knife; furtive, in haste, he strips off
the splashed ceremonial garments;

      the charwoman who scrubs
off the stone of the altar; the man who rakes up
the widow's ashes, handfuls of bone
in the embers of wood;

      those who dispose

of the dreadful torso when the decree
to dismember has been carried out
and the crowd dispersed; who come in with a hose
to rinse the charnel house floor;
                              those who sweep up
what is left of the monk
who clothed himself in the fiery robes
of protest at the command post gates;
                              those who glean
after the harvest, permitted to gather
what remains, who leave the killing fields
with a small box and a stone
in the throat, a silence
that nothing will ever dislodge;
                              those who are
heart-scalded, digging the mass graves,
tipping the barrows into the trenches;
                              those who clean the tiles
of the mosque after the bomb
took the man at his prayers, who lie down
but find peace gone from their sleep;
                              all those who come after
the drama is over, all those who
have seen.

2.

Now, with you, Sujata, we see it:
how the elephants, swaying, walk away
from the compounds, how they follow
tracks in the dust to a watering place
where, in a time of drought, the animals trek
miles to the shores of a distant lake
that, however shrunken, still fills
from an underground source, and there—
among deer and white rhinos, hyena,
wild horses, leopard and lion—the elephants
stand at the lake's edge and see,
looking back, a congress of eyes
like the tail of the peacock
outspread, alive in the water; the eyes
waver and shimmer, then
swim off like minnows
as the ancient ones enter
their own breaking image,
bend their gray heads, and drink.

•     •     •

Sujata, perhaps you are thinking of this
as you stand at the bathroom sink
that has replaced the communal fountain;
perhaps you are thinking of this
as you splash water into your burning eyes—
black eyes that keep vision safe
from the glaring sun, but whose pigment
is no shield against atrocity; the eye,
scorched, taking it in,
returns it, bathed in the cool

waters of reflection, the way
you fill your cupped hands with water,
running cold from the metal faucet
in this Northern town—and now, no,
I don't know what you think, wouldn't
presume, but I know how it feels
as the cool water bathes your tired eyes,
as the same water floods mine,
from the headwaters of that Nile
no traveler has found,
the waters that are falling forever
down the cliff on whose edge
we find ourselves, staring together
into the endless gray, and feeling
on our skin, in our eyes, the fine
atomized silk of its spray.

# *Moonsnails*

—a poem for Susan

The size, you said, of silver dollars
but then, the weight is wrong, for these
aren't solid things at all—the snail
mere water, the silver case a streak
of moon, of light that curls
where little perturbations of the tidal
pools send water in its spiral
tracks on which the moonlight writes,
the no man's land between
the wild tides and the stiff resistance
of the human world...here
the mudsnails snooze and dream,
while the moonsnails lie
like cast-off trails of glory
on the black mysterious backs
of secret pools, and when the sea
has pulled away, gone so far out
the pools forget the daily
maelstroms of the tides
that, as they slide in, open
a million mouths of shell
hinged to the water's flow; when all this
hunger seems a dream, the mouths
all shut, the clams burrowed back in the silt,
not a frond stirring—then the moon

comes down to lie
on the black satin skin
of the pool, in love with life
in its shallow bed, for a moment,
a perfect round, so absolute, so
fragile that the merest breath
exhaled on the sky's dark mirror
will set the silver
wavering, then illusion's
perfect circle,
shuddering, is gone,
and, in its place, moonsnails,
the shining, silver spirals
of the breath unshelled,
 turning in and out until
      the tidal flats are moiré silks,
   wind makes the ghostly moonsnails
swim and shimmer in the pools
      on night's reflected shore,
 out there, stars swim in the wide black
         pool of space, mere shallows to
                         the space beyond
the black night spinning out of itself
            trails of light that disappear
      into that distance
where no horizon is, where
   the universe is going out, everywhere
at once     moonsnails glimmer, spiral galaxies that spin
                  on the trackless waters where the veils
                  of the primordial fire hang
                        at the red edge
                        of sight

God, for a silver dollar in the hand,
cool heft of metal from the earth's
sweet veins, or a real moonsnail,
a tiny dish of light, but solid,
dreamless, curled inside—
its artless slice of life.

# *Freed from Another Context*

—for Francine

1.

Here, the foreground of the other
side, and she is watching
raptors float across the blue
ground of the sky—hawk, eagle,
osprey, owl; seized from afar,
she holds the vision in the field glass
of a farseeing eye, focused, extended,
as only the practiced eye can be,
years spent looking out, scanning
the horizon for a speck, staring at a bleak
expanse of sea, learning to interpret
every dot—a flash of fish, a falling
boy, a ship. Or if the house is set
on plains, on the cold griddle
where the glacier had its way,
the watch is lonelier still,
the hope longer, attenuated as
the freight trains stretched across
the darkened land, one line of light
to interrupt night's solid blank.

She watches with the raptor's eye,
trained on distance as she is,
and dark—so when she turns
to what is close, so intimate
and huge, she keeps the gift
of sight beyond herself,
neither sentimental nor detached.


2.

Look—a patch of snow, afloat,
the owl!

Below, soul's
shadow on the lawn; a warmth
that will not leave the hand.


3.

There is resemblance, and its sense:
the silver alive at the back
of the mirror; the fishing bird
who must find its catch
through the cast of its own shadow.

Everything moves another
thing, and that in another
way—the leaves on the oak
stir the air like oars, the fish
on the weathervane turns the wind
way around to the south, and the flight
of the owl rouses the moon
whose face on the water
awakens her, and the floor
of the world is desire's sky—
familiar feathers brush her
cheek, wings flicker
in her blood,
              and the head of the owl
swivels all the way round
till the moon's dark side
swims up from the pond,
and she sees from
the other side.

# Remedios Varo as Daphne

Inside the rooms are tall, begin to open;
    the walls, the ceilings rustle; there is
        a moon caught in the mirror of the dark
            wine in the crystal bowl, where, through one
                jagged hole, the night stares in; vine leaves
            whisper on the walls; a few, torn loose,
        scuttle across the floor; the walls breathe;
    they are like a bellows, an integument,
translucent, osmotic; rains dampen
    them, they weep; in the wet cracked glass
        of the skylight, the night sky flickers
            like a guttering lamp; from the unraveling
                strands of woven roof, stars dangle;
            and from the floor, where the old mosaics
        crumble and crack, slender shoots, gray-green,
    poke through; a small stream splashes
over the faces, gilt and lapis, of the tiled
    fish; the ribbon of water winds shining
        through the trunks of trees that rise
            from the figured carpet of the floor: wind-
        flowers, leaves worked by larvae
    into a delicate lace, violets, the fingertip
touch of ferns, the sheen on the leaves
    of laurel, its bark swelling, as if

the river's daughter, Daphne, would
unlock from deep inside it,
        and so, unrooted, laughing,
    walk again the stones, gnat-adorned
and damp, where you can hear the roar of
waterfalls pouring from high cliffs
into the pools that feed the streams
where, sun-struck, the salmon leap
    toward home. The river slides along
        beside her, as she picks her way
            downstream. She stoops
    to choose some pebbles, throws
    the small white stones, like dice,
on to the current; they skip across
the water—distant doves,
    they lift and flutter off.
        She watches, empty-handed, turns
        and sees, along the river, how
            the banks are crowded with laurels—
    bushes barely started, striplings, full grown
    trees: everywhere she looks, the laurels.
They are moving, like a tide, down from
the hillsides, from the higher slopes,
    rolling boulders aside, stirring up snakes,
        pushing through the underbrush; on every side
        she hears the rustling as of skirts,
            the sound of torn roots trailing
    over ground. As a bird will pick its notes
    from the other voices raised
in chorus, so she takes heart from them.

At home in the place recovered
        from the fruitless time of legend,
                Grail quest, greenwood and Garden,
                        the thousand Arcadys of man's desire—
                here in the daylit clearing, the sun
            warming her still damp limbs, she is
        standing, picking leaves from her hair, laughing
as she throws them to the current,
        watching as they lift, and turn
                in spirals, move off toward
                        where the river hastens
                                to the next great fall:    tomorrow


                                over whose lip
                                    no one can see—
                                only mist
                                and a welter
                                of water

# The Mulch

—for Sujata and Michael and Jenny Mira


Leaning on the gold
of autumn is how it starts,
first the light in the gingko's
yellow leaves, then the breeze
that sets them moving
like the gold in the hold
of a Spanish galleon as it falls
slowly through the waves,
spilling its hammered bits of coin
that turn as they fall with a riffle
of light, almost a school of plated
fish, flickering through the half-
light of the undersea, before it
gets so deep, so close to winter,
that all the leaves have fallen,
the gold settled to the bottom
in the silt, turned by the rains
and the icy sleet, the layers
of damp of day after day, into
a gray amorphous mass
in which those bulbous creatures
move, segmented, smooth,
like the insides of some higher
beast, the part earth hides away

inside, or under leaves, recoils
around these slugs, the blind, unthinking
ropes on which the soil depends.
As golden leaf turns slowly into mulch,
spring tugs the stem, it rises
from the pond's deep mud; its dark green
pads, like leather wings on some prehistoric
bird still tied to water, spread out
around it, and the great bud
lifts like a pair of praying
hands, begins to open in a slow pink
spray of silk—each blossom
large as a human head, and swaying,
securely fastened on its stem;
in its center, outlandish dancing
cone, its apex down
like a spinning top
but still
inside
its seeds will start it all
again—from where they feed
on fallen gold, on fall,
when turning leaves
ripe with light
sift down around
the lotus
whose blossom rises
from deep within the mind
where, out of all we thought
forgotten,
love
prepared the flower.

# Recantation

We look down at our hands, scratched
and blistered from digging through
the smoldering rubble
of the past, its dream: that we shall be
raised high. And they who cast us
in the pit shall come to us and beg,
for a handful of seed, a crust of bread.

Alive, under a veil so thick
that even pressing it we couldn't feel
the shape of what lay, pulsing, underneath—
who were these enemies? Their names,
like faces on a stream, break up
and change with every breeze.

Centuries of drought; the line of
lean cows stands to the horizon's rim,
while seeds in the metal silos rot.
Thunder rumbles; distance flickers
on and off, the rain sends its first few
drops. And we are helpless
to do more than welcome
the downpour when it comes—
to shed our clothes and feel
its cool tongue slide along
our dusty skin, as a mare will lick
her foal, newborn and still
half-shawled in the garnet world
within, until it rises, unsteady,
its eyes open, blinking at the brilliance
of the startled light—
                        we, who thought
to seed the clouds and make
earth fill our fields with grain
and see the sheaves bow down
to us in gratitude like gods;
we, who were just children
wrapped in the deep-dyed fabric
of a father's dream.

# *Kazuko's Vision*

In the blizzard's heart,
a little girl lies stretched out
on the snow, watching the sky repeat
itself in white, each flake a petal
from a cherry tree, Heaven's *Sakura*,
the great tree larger than the compass
of the eye; the snowflakes blur, obscure
the bridge that Hiroshige veiled with bits
of white, the same snow falls tonight: for time—
our little minutes, hours, histories,
small as the holes a pin makes
in a shoji screen—has broken
loose, and floating on the breeze's
back, drifts in the swing
of cool black air, night's loosened
hair whose sheen is like the sea
on a night when the moon is full, its
glitter scattered on black waves…
just so, the snow, as it spills from space,
floats easily, the way birds
ride the wind, look down and see
one small figure in a red
snowsuit, floating in a field
of white, and looking

up, laughing as the snowflakes fill
her eyes, her mind, the sky—until it's all
one thing: sky, self and snow, a host
of almost-same, untied, afloat
together in a dance of wind
and breath...so, one by one
by one, things fade
into each other and the snow
makes night a weightless space
where centuries
lightly pass, vanishing
like snowflakes
falling
on a lake.

# American Painting, with Rain

The gates have closed to the rotted park,
amusements rusted in the rain,
the roller-coaster curve turns out
toward sea, and there the rails are
broken off, the structure hangs
in air, like wires
from a ruptured wall.

The hour grows late, the dark comes down;
the animals are wading to the ark. The day
is sinking as the waters rise; you hear
the plash of deer, of buffalo, of wolf,
who walk together, heads down,
in the thick downpour, their hides wet,
the heavy smell rising like steam,
leaving the place deserted,
a promontory view
of gray and swelling sea.

For years the English painters
composed their seascapes looking in
toward land, the ocean in the foreground,
the horizon home, the island anchoring the eye.
But here, from America, the artist,
looking out, makes the foreground land,
the horizon is the waiting sea,
its inescapable heave,
the distance crying like a hidden
baby in the night, calling out,
a promise of tomorrow, or...
The gulls circle and
scream. Something is torn.

Standing here, at the edge of the canvas,
the brush fallen, the waves crawling
over the edge of the frame, eating
away at even the notion of art,
the gray frame houses on the coast
giving way to mold and the storms
of too many winters, and the view
out there with too many waves, the sea
an infinite set of perspectives, no end
in sight, distance pouring back at us
from everywhere we look,
until vision itself is a sieve
letting the waters in, even here
in this room, safe
under the artifical lights, sure
of the concrete floor under our feet,
we feel the slow lapping of water
at our ankles, its wet crawl
toward our calves, the rising chill

as we slog toward the exit, as we move,
with the animals, wading out,
as fast as we dare through the growing
dark, and the rain, the unknown
terrain, the obstructions we can only guess
as we collide with them, their shapes disguised
in sheets of water, collecting shadows,
the uncertain lights.

As an actor fades
behind a scrim when the lights
dim—figures, walking slowly into
curtains of rain, seem oddly
not to walk away at all, but simply to
dissolve into the dot matrix
of the mist. This is not the ending we
would have chosen, trained, as we were,
in the old way, the clear outline,
the bold stroke, the lucid use
of perspective, hard light,
strong shadows,
the single
vanishing
point.

•

In Hawai'i the rain comes down hard,
friendly, the forest is used to it,
the flowers in their profusion
a perennial thirst. A woman stands
in the open doorway of her house,
dreaming of Maine, of thunder and
the leaves of the maple turning

to face familiar weather. But the child
has never known anything but
the rains of Hawai'i, its trees
laden with blossoms, the stars
in the night sky so much like
the small white sweet flowers
in the dark green hedge by the door
that the heavens too must be
perfumed to the very edge
of infinitude—he doesn't yet
think these things but he is filled
with them, all the same. He stands,
leaning toward the falling water,
holding his mother's leg
for support, this little
Noah, untroubled
by the freight his name carries,
small steward of the future,
loving these rains, seeing
only the shining veils
of his bridal with
the world, standing
on the rim of the Pacific
on his island that is all of earth
to him, boundless, secure,
standing on the threshold of
the house of Sarah and Matthew,
greeting the rain.

# Changing the Imperatives

And having remembered it, then—
what next? Oh, go ahead, they said, lift
the stone of memory from the heart
like the stone from the mouth
of the tomb. And are they to blame
for what stumbles out, rags
crawling with maggots and lice, into
the blinding day?

Listen, my friend, they gave you
the key to the wrong door,
the one marked Sins of the Fathers—
the one that opens onto the abyss
where obsession hangs its ladder
over the lip, where the dead
climb daily back up out of the gulf
dragging their broken bones, each day
more ruined than the one before,
until, nearly spent,
they are little more than handfuls
of powder, aroused like genies
by the slightest wind, resentful dust
that keeps the air
unbreathable.

The past. The wretched luck that,
nailed to the mast, becomes the goad
for which the ship is lost.
Take up the fallen hammer
and turning it around, pry
the nail from Ahab's gold doubloon,
then toss it over the side.
Watch how fast the ocean can forget,
how brief an opening your entry
makes, how soon the wave
shuts back upon itself, how small
a curiosity the turning bit of gold
excites as it drifts down
through the endless sift of green . . .
years later when the salvage men
dredge up the sand, they'll find
only a disc of gold, round
as the old threshing floors
of Crete, but small enough
to fit into the hand; the face
it wore—unrecognizable.
Then drill a hole and wear it
on a ribbon as a talisman,
relic of the gentle, veiled power—
forgetfulness, the goddess
whose name nobody knows,
whose shrines are forgotten,
her temples overgrown,
her images lost.

# Notes

1. "Night Fishing in the Sound": The echo of "cauldron of dawn" with Sylvia Plath's "cauldron of morning" at the end of "Ariel" was not intended, and may have been merely coincidental. But if it is an echo, however subconscious, I acknowledge the debt.

2. "Being as I Was, How Could I Help...": The dance "Cry Wolf," choreographed for Zero Moving by its founding director, Hellmut Gottschild, has been growing and changing over the years. It was the latest and most moving incarnation, performed in 1991, including a visual reference to the Lupercalian Wolf who suckled Romulus and Remus, that engendered this poem.

3. "When Asked to Lie Down on the Altar": This poem was written in immediate response to reading Marie's Howe's poem "Isaac" in *The Good Thief* (Persea Books, 1988).

4. "*Ume*: Plum": The pronunciation of *ume* sounds the final *e*—*oo-meh*. *Sakura* means both cherry tree and cherry blossom.

5. "Recurrence in Another Tongue" began with a literal translation from the Russian of "Tristia" by Vadim Erent. My attempt at an English version soon turned into a variation, and finally into a new poem spoken by the posthumous but felt presence of Osip Mandelstam—a presence, I am convinced, called up by Vadim, Mandelstam's young compatriot in the art of poetry and in impassioned dissent.

Nadezdha, the name of Mandelstam's wife, also means "hope" in Russian.

6. "The Walls" was originally written, in a longer version, as text for a dance performance piece of Melanie Stewart Dance called "Barriers," which was made in collaboration with Melanie Stewart as choreographer and John Mitchell as composer.

7. "The Muse": The Lacan of this poem refers, to be unfair, to a French theorist who has confused symbol making with the discovery of a certain part of the male anatomy. He, along with his secondary and tertiary hordes of redactors, is currently enjoying a vogue in the Academy in the criticism and replacement of literature by a set of abstruse encoded signals, somewhat like those elaborately patterned clouds of smoke once reputed to have been sent through skillful flapping of blankets to distant members of one's tribe.

8. "The Lament of the Valkyrie": The line in the eighth stanza, "the crimson web of war," is from the refrain line of the poem "The Fatal Sisters" (1761) by the English poet Thomas Gray.

9. "...as soft and as pink as a nursery..." is from the lyrics to the song "The Girl That I Marry," sung in a booming bass by Howard Keel, a big beefy soporific movie star, in the film version of "Annie Get Your Gun."

10. "The Secret Garden": This poem owes its existence to a story told me by Carlen Arnett about a man who thinks that women have a secret (possibly a secret garden), and that they are keeping it from men.

11. "Those Who Come After" owes its precipitating thought to Mary Kinzie. We were speaking of the power of the Greek myths, still enlivening after all these centuries, when she suddenly cast herself into a future where a similar conversation might be taking place, and said, more or less in these words: "No one will ever say of us, what wonderful myths they had."

12. "What Was Left Over": This poem addresses itself to a poem by Sujata Bhatt, "What Happened to the Elephant?," in her book *Monkey Shadows* (Carcanet Press, 1991).

13. "Moonsnails" was born of my misreading of a poem by Susan Roney-O'Brien about mudsnails, which I took to be "moonsnails," that is, the snail-like silver patterns that moonlight makes on tidal pools. My poem rides on and then tries to recover from that mistake.

14. "Kazuko's Vision": The vision of this poem was told to me by Kazuko Terada, a former student in Tokyo, of an actual childhood experience, vividly recalled. What I did not expect was that in the retelling of it, it would form for me an image of the Japanese flag transformed into a little girl in a red snowsuit dreaming in a field of snow, which is how the experience of living in Japan humanized that emblem for me.

15. "Remedios Varo as Daphne": Remedios Varo (1908–62) was a Spanish painter who expatriated to Mexico during World War II. The images of the first twenty-four lines or so of the poem are largely descriptive of a magical painting of hers called "To Be Reborn" (1960), though the images are really composites drawn from a number of her paintings. The book which brings together her work and her life, and is responsible for my sense of her importance in turning the woman from the changed (Daphne) into the changer (the woman artist/alchemist), is *Unexpected Journeys* by Janet A. Kaplan (Abbeville Press, 1988).

16. "American Painting, with Rain": The Sarah and Matthew of the poem are not just emblems: they are friends Sarah Lantz and Matthew Woodside whom I visited in Hawai'i. And Noah is the name of their small son.